How Not to
FORGET
EVERYTHING

A Weekly Planner for Those with Toddlers

Activinotes

DAILY JOURNALS, PLANNERS, NOTEBOOKS AND OTHER BLANK BOOKS

Copyright 2016

Weekly Planner

Weekly Planner

MONDAY	TUESDAY	WEDNESDAY

Afternoon Schedules

THURSDAY	To Do List	Notes

Afternoon Schedules

Weekly Planner

FRIDAY	SATURDAY	SUNDAY

Afternoon Schedules

Notes

To Do List

Weekly Planner

MONDAY	TUESDAY	WEDNESDAY

Afternoon Schedules

THURSDAY	To Do List	Notes

Afternoon Schedules

Weekly Planner

FRIDAY	SATURDAY	SUNDAY

Afternoon Schedules

Notes

To Do List

Weekly Planner

_____

_____

_____

_____

_____

_____

_____

_____

_____

_____

_____

_____

_____

_____

_____

_____

_____

_____

_____

Weekly Planner

Weekly Planner

MONDAY	TUESDAY	WEDNESDAY

Afternoon Schedules

THURSDAY	To Do List	Notes

Afternoon Schedules

Weekly Planner

FRIDAY	SATURDAY	SUNDAY

Afternoon Schedules

Notes

To Do List

Weekly Planner

MONDAY	TUESDAY	WEDNESDAY

Afternoon Schedules

THURSDAY	To Do List	Notes

Afternoon Schedules

Weekly Planner

FRIDAY	SATURDAY	SUNDAY

Afternoon Schedules

Notes

To Do List

Weekly Planner

Weekly Planner

_____

_____

_____

_____

_____

_____

_____

_____

_____

_____

_____

_____

_____

_____

_____

_____

Weekly Planner

MONDAY	TUESDAY	WEDNESDAY

Afternoon Schedules

THURSDAY	To Do List	Notes

Afternoon Schedules

Weekly Planner

FRIDAY	SATURDAY	SUNDAY

Afternoon Schedules

Notes

To Do List

Weekly Planner

MONDAY	TUESDAY	WEDNESDAY

Afternoon Schedules

THURSDAY	To Do List	Notes

Afternoon Schedules

Weekly Planner

FRIDAY	SATURDAY	SUNDAY

Afternoon Schedules

FRIDAY	SATURDAY	SUNDAY

Notes

To Do List

Weekly Planner

Weekly Planner

Weekly Planner

MONDAY	TUESDAY	WEDNESDAY

Afternoon Schedules

THURSDAY	To Do List	Notes

Afternoon Schedules

Weekly Planner

FRIDAY	SATURDAY	SUNDAY

Afternoon Schedules

Notes

To Do List

Weekly Planner

MONDAY	TUESDAY	WEDNESDAY

Afternoon Schedules

THURSDAY	To Do List	Notes

Afternoon Schedules

Weekly Planner

FRIDAY	SATURDAY	SUNDAY

Afternoon Schedules

Notes

To Do List

Weekly Planner

Weekly Planner

_____

_____

_____

_____

_____

_____

_____

_____

_____

_____

_____

_____

_____

_____

_____

_____

_____

Weekly Planner

MONDAY	TUESDAY	WEDNESDAY

Afternoon Schedules

THURSDAY	To Do List	Notes

Afternoon Schedules

Weekly Planner

FRIDAY	SATURDAY	SUNDAY

Afternoon Schedules

Notes

To Do List

Weekly Planner

MONDAY	TUESDAY	WEDNESDAY

Afternoon Schedules

THURSDAY	To Do List	Notes

Afternoon Schedules

Weekly Planner

FRIDAY	SATURDAY	SUNDAY

Afternoon Schedules

Notes

To Do List

Weekly Planner

Weekly Planner

Weekly Planner

MONDAY	TUESDAY	WEDNESDAY

Afternoon Schedules

THURSDAY	To Do List	Notes

Afternoon Schedules

Weekly Planner

FRIDAY	SATURDAY	SUNDAY

Afternoon Schedules

Notes

To Do List

Weekly Planner

MONDAY	TUESDAY	WEDNESDAY

Afternoon Schedules

THURSDAY	To Do List	Notes

Afternoon Schedules

Weekly Planner

FRIDAY	SATURDAY	SUNDAY

Afternoon Schedules

Notes

To Do List

Weekly Planner

_____
_____
_____
_____
_____
_____
_____
_____
_____
_____
_____
_____
_____
_____
_____
_____
_____
_____

Weekly Planner

Weekly Planner

MONDAY	TUESDAY	WEDNESDAY

Afternoon Schedules

THURSDAY	To Do List	Notes

Afternoon Schedules

Weekly Planner

FRIDAY	SATURDAY	SUNDAY

Afternoon Schedules

Notes

To Do List

Weekly Planner

MONDAY	TUESDAY	WEDNESDAY

Afternoon Schedules

THURSDAY	To Do List	Notes

Afternoon Schedules

Weekly Planner

FRIDAY	SATURDAY	SUNDAY

Afternoon Schedules

FRIDAY	SATURDAY	SUNDAY

Notes

To Do List

Weekly Planner

Weekly Planner

Weekly Planner

MONDAY	TUESDAY	WEDNESDAY

Afternoon Schedules

THURSDAY	To Do List	Notes

Afternoon Schedules

Weekly Planner

FRIDAY	SATURDAY	SUNDAY

Afternoon Schedules

Notes

To Do List

Weekly Planner

MONDAY	TUESDAY	WEDNESDAY

Afternoon Schedules

THURSDAY	To Do List	Notes

Afternoon Schedules

Weekly Planner

FRIDAY	SATURDAY	SUNDAY

Afternoon Schedules

Notes

To Do List

Weekly Planner

_____

_____

_____

_____

_____

_____

_____

_____

_____

_____

_____

_____

_____

_____

_____

_____

_____

_____

Weekly Planner

Weekly Planner

MONDAY	TUESDAY	WEDNESDAY

Afternoon Schedules

THURSDAY	To Do List	Notes

Afternoon Schedules

Weekly Planner

FRIDAY	SATURDAY	SUNDAY

Afternoon Schedules

Notes

To Do List

Weekly Planner

MONDAY	TUESDAY	WEDNESDAY

Afternoon Schedules

THURSDAY	To Do List	Notes

Afternoon Schedules

Weekly Planner

FRIDAY	SATURDAY	SUNDAY

Afternoon Schedules

Notes

To Do List

Weekly Planner

Weekly Planner

_____

_____

_____

_____

_____

_____

_____

_____

_____

_____

_____

_____

_____

_____

_____

_____

_____

Weekly Planner

MONDAY	TUESDAY	WEDNESDAY

Afternoon Schedules

THURSDAY	To Do List	Notes

Afternoon Schedules

Weekly Planner

FRIDAY	SATURDAY	SUNDAY

Afternoon Schedules

Notes

To Do List

Weekly Planner

MONDAY	TUESDAY	WEDNESDAY

Afternoon Schedules

THURSDAY	To Do List	Notes

Afternoon Schedules

Weekly Planner

FRIDAY	SATURDAY	SUNDAY

Afternoon Schedules

Notes

To Do List

Weekly Planner

Weekly Planner

Weekly Planner

MONDAY	TUESDAY	WEDNESDAY

Afternoon Schedules

THURSDAY	To Do List	Notes

Afternoon Schedules

Weekly Planner

FRIDAY	SATURDAY	SUNDAY

Afternoon Schedules

Notes

To Do List

Weekly Planner

MONDAY	TUESDAY	WEDNESDAY

Afternoon Schedules

THURSDAY	To Do List	Notes

Afternoon Schedules

Weekly Planner

FRIDAY	SATURDAY	SUNDAY

Afternoon Schedules

Notes

To Do List

Weekly Planner

Weekly Planner

Weekly Planner

MONDAY	TUESDAY	WEDNESDAY

Afternoon Schedules

THURSDAY	To Do List	Notes

Afternoon Schedules

Weekly Planner

FRIDAY	SATURDAY	SUNDAY

Afternoon Schedules

Notes

To Do List

Weekly Planner

MONDAY	TUESDAY	WEDNESDAY

Afternoon Schedules

THURSDAY	To Do List	Notes

Afternoon Schedules

Weekly Planner

FRIDAY	SATURDAY	SUNDAY

Afternoon Schedules

Notes

To Do List

Weekly Planner

_____

_____

_____

_____

_____

_____

_____

_____

_____

_____

_____

_____

_____

_____

_____

_____

_____

Weekly Planner

Weekly Planner

MONDAY	TUESDAY	WEDNESDAY

Afternoon Schedules

THURSDAY	To Do List	Notes

Afternoon Schedules

Weekly Planner

FRIDAY	SATURDAY	SUNDAY

Afternoon Schedules

Notes

To Do List

Weekly Planner

MONDAY	TUESDAY	WEDNESDAY

Afternoon Schedules

THURSDAY	To Do List	Notes

Afternoon Schedules

Weekly Planner

FRIDAY	SATURDAY	SUNDAY

Afternoon Schedules

Notes

To Do List

Weekly Planner

_____
_____
_____
_____
_____
_____
_____
_____
_____
_____
_____
_____
_____
_____
_____
_____
_____
_____

Weekly Planner

_____

_____

_____

_____

_____

_____

_____

_____

_____

_____

_____

_____

_____

_____

_____

_____

Weekly Planner

MONDAY	TUESDAY	WEDNESDAY

Afternoon Schedules

THURSDAY	To Do List	Notes

Afternoon Schedules

Weekly Planner

FRIDAY	SATURDAY	SUNDAY

Afternoon Schedules

Notes

To Do List

Weekly Planner

MONDAY	TUESDAY	WEDNESDAY

Afternoon Schedules

THURSDAY	To Do List	Notes

Afternoon Schedules

Weekly Planner

FRIDAY	SATURDAY	SUNDAY

Afternoon Schedules

Notes

To Do List

Weekly Planner

_____
_____
_____
_____
_____
_____
_____
_____
_____
_____
_____
_____
_____
_____
_____
_____
_____
_____

Weekly Planner

Weekly Planner

MONDAY	TUESDAY	WEDNESDAY

Afternoon Schedules

THURSDAY	To Do List	Notes
Afternoon Schedules		

Weekly Planner

FRIDAY	SATURDAY	SUNDAY

Afternoon Schedules

Notes

To Do List

Weekly Planner

MONDAY	TUESDAY	WEDNESDAY

Afternoon Schedules

THURSDAY	To Do List	Notes

Afternoon Schedules

Weekly Planner

FRIDAY	SATURDAY	SUNDAY

Afternoon Schedules

Notes

To Do List

Weekly Planner

_____

_____

_____

_____

_____

_____

_____

_____

_____

_____

_____

_____

_____

_____

_____

_____

_____

_____

Weekly Planner

Weekly Planner

MONDAY	TUESDAY	WEDNESDAY

Afternoon Schedules

THURSDAY	To Do List	Notes

Afternoon Schedules

Weekly Planner

FRIDAY	SATURDAY	SUNDAY

Afternoon Schedules

Notes

To Do List

Weekly Planner

MONDAY	TUESDAY	WEDNESDAY

Afternoon Schedules

THURSDAY	To Do List	Notes

Afternoon Schedules

Weekly Planner

FRIDAY	SATURDAY	SUNDAY

Afternoon Schedules

Notes

To Do List

Weekly Planner

Weekly Planner

Weekly Planner

MONDAY	TUESDAY	WEDNESDAY

Afternoon Schedules

THURSDAY	To Do List	Notes
Afternoon Schedules		

Weekly Planner

FRIDAY	SATURDAY	SUNDAY

Afternoon Schedules

Notes

To Do List

Weekly Planner

MONDAY	TUESDAY	WEDNESDAY

Afternoon Schedules

THURSDAY	To Do List	Notes

Afternoon Schedules

Weekly Planner

FRIDAY	SATURDAY	SUNDAY

Afternoon Schedules

Notes

To Do List

Weekly Planner

Weekly Planner

www.ingramcontent.com/pod-product-compliance
Lightning Source LLC
Chambersburg PA
CBHW081334090426
42737CB00017B/3141